IMAGES
of America

SAUGERTIES

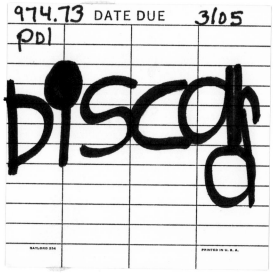

The scenic Esopus Creek falls and dam, photographed in 1893, which provided waterpower for industry in Saugerties.

IMAGES
of America

SAUGERTIES

Edward Poll and Karlyn Knaust Elia

ARCADIA

First published 1997
Copyright © Edward Poll and Karlyn Knaust Elia, 1997

ISBN 0-7524-0853-4

Published by Arcadia Publishing,
an imprint of the Chalford Publishing Corporation,
One Washington Center, Dover, New Hampshire 03820.
Printed in Great Britain

Library of Congress Cataloging-in-Publication Data applied for

Contents

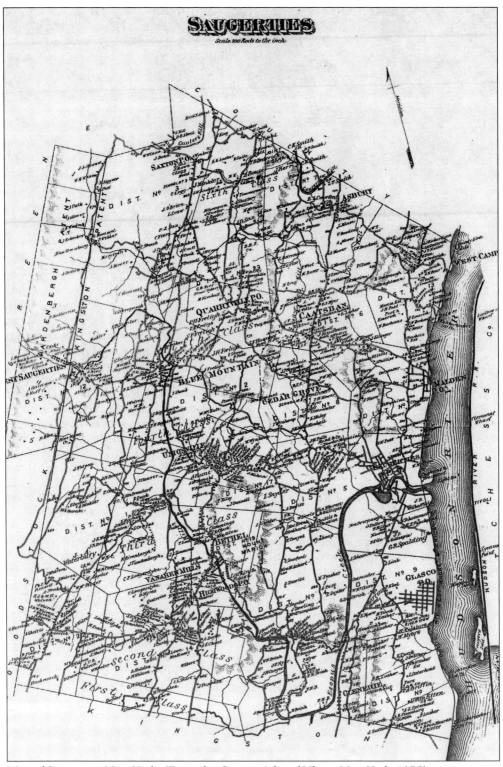

Map of Saugerties, New York. (From the *County Atlas of Ulster, New York*, 1875).

Introduction

Saugerties, New York, has the distinction of possessing a name unlike any other community's. The name Saugerties is believed to be a version of an old Dutch word meaning "sawyer," or one who operates a sawmill. The first land granted to a white settler in this area, described as "lands along the river and to the blue mountains beyond," was known as a part of Rennsselaerswyck. The grant included Sawyer's Kill, where Barent Cornelius Volge, the original "Little Sawyer," erected a sawmill before 1663. In the decades that followed, permanent settlers of the town arrived and were led by Cornelius Lambertson Brink (1688) and Petrus Winnie (1700).

Saugerties, although unique in name, had many similarities with developing towns along the Hudson River in the nineteenth century. Situated between the Catskill Mountains on its western border and more than 8 miles of river shoreline on its eastern border, Saugerties began as a typical Hudson River town. Industry depended on the great waterway for commerce. Saugerties' natural resources made it an industrial boomtown in the nineteenth century. From Saugerties came brick, bluestone, paper, lead, iron, ice, and produce. The numerous tiny hamlets throughout the town bear witness to the various industries that developed within them.

West Camp was the site of the immigration of a significant number of German Palatines under the auspices of the British government in 1710. Many of their descendants remain in Saugerties today. In the nineteenth century, Irish, English, and Welsh immigrants came to work in the developing paper, iron, and lead mills along the Esopus Creek, and the bluestone quarries in the hamlets of Quarryville, High Woods, and Fish Creek. Italian immigrants came to the hamlet of Glasco to work in the brickyards in the late nineteenth century. In the twentieth century, refugees came to Saugerties from the Baltic states after World War II.

The history of Saugerties is reflected in the pages of this book, a photographic history. Both professional and amateur photographers have made a visual record of the people, places, and events in historic Saugerties.

Most of the photographic images in this book have been contributed by townspeople. Their willingness to share their stories and their history is an example of their neighborliness and pride. The authors wish to extend thanks to Jean Wrolsen, Francis Wolven, Seward R. Osborne, Vernon A. Benjamin, Louis Francello, Harry McCarthy, Rayann Fatizzi, Robert Wade, Jean Graber Poll, and Alex Wade. The authors would like to extend special thanks to their families for their patience and support.

We hope you will enjoy these images of Saugerties and want to learn more of its history. Welcome to "Friendly Saugerties."

One

The Hudson River
and the Esopus Creek

The Saugerties Lighthouse on the Hudson River at the mouth of the Esopus Creek, 1950. An earlier lighthouse built in 1835 used whale oil lamps to guide river traffic. In 1869, the present lighthouse was constructed by the Lighthouse Establishment. The lighthouse had a beacon light and a bell to help ships locate their position in darkness and fog. The Saugerties Lighthouse was one of a string of lighthouses spaced along the river. A great waterway extended from the Great Lakes through the Erie Canal to the Hudson River and finally to the Atlantic Ocean. (Photograph by Dick Smith.)

The *Clermont* (North River steamboat) replica, 1909. In 1807, Robert Fulton's *Clermont* made its landmark voyage under steam power from New York to Albany. Its captain was Andrew Brink of Saugerties. Many people scoffed at the idea of a steam-powered ship and nicknamed the boat "Fulton's Folly." They thought the steamboat would never work and that sailing ships like sloops and schooners would never be replaced. The *Clermont*'s success ushered in the era of steam-powered ships. (From *The Hudson-Fulton Celebration*, 1909.)

The explosion of the *Reindeer*, 1852. The steamboat *Reindeer* left New York City sailing for Albany with three hundred passengers aboard. After docking at Bristol (now Malden-on-Hudson), a hamlet in Saugerties, the steam boiler exploded, killing thirty-six people. The *New York Times* reported that the injured, scalded, and burned victims were taken to the Malden Hotel and the Exchange Hotel. A lyrical lament describing the catastrophe was written in 1852 by Henry Backus, the "Saugerties Bard." (Saugerties Town Historian.)

The *Ansonia*, docked on the Lower Esopus, 1875. Built in 1848, the *Ansonia* first worked the route connecting New York City and Derby, Connecticut. During the Civil War, the steamer helped transport Union troops. *Ansonia* began service for the New York and Saugerties Transportation Company in the spring of 1865, making three trips per week between Saugerties and New York. The Saugerties steamboats were primarily night boats, sailing in the evening and arriving in the morning. *Ansonia* was reconstructed and renamed twice. In 1891 *Ansonia* was purchased by the newly formed Saugerties and New York Steamboat Company. The boat was lengthened and renamed *Ulster*. In turn, the *Ulster* was converted and renamed *Robert A. Snyder* in 1920. Plying the Hudson for over sixty-five years, this ship was Saugerties' longest running steamship. (Photograph by Edward Jernegan from *The Pearl*.)

The *Saugerties*, Esopus Creek, *c.* 1900. The *Saugerties* began its overnight journeys to New York City in 1889. The one-way trip took from seven to nine hours depending on the tides and the wind. "Travel by night and save a day," was the slogan. Passengers could watch the Hudson River scenery, eat dinner, and socialize. In the summertime a band was sometimes aboard for entertainment. The stops along the way were at Tivoli, Barrytown, Ulster Landing, and Rhinecliff. (Saugerties Town Historian.)

November 22, 1903. On this date, a fire aboard the *Saugerties* burned out of control and gutted the ship at its dock. The burned ship remained in the Esopus Creek, and many onlookers came to examine the wreckage. Later, the *Saugerties* was floated out to the flats north of the lighthouse, and the slow process of disintegration began. (Courtesy of Don Curry.)

The *Ulster*, c. 1905. The *Ansonia* was refitted in 1892 and renamed *Ulster*. The ship was lengthened to 205 feet, and the freeboard increased so the steamer would float higher in the water. The ship had forty staterooms providing private overnight accommodations. There were separate cabin berths for men and women. Like the other Saugerties steamboats, *Ulster* was a "side wheeler," with circular paddle wheels on each side of the ship. (Hudson River Maritime Museum Collection.)

November 11, 1887. The *Ulster* ran aground on this night at the base of Storm King Mountain. The *Ulster*'s bow edged within a few feet of the West Shore Railroad tracks. No one was seriously injured. The shaken passengers walked to the nearest railroad station and continued their journey by train. (Hudson River Maritime Museum Collection.)

A birthday party for Robert A. Snyder, center front row holding a bouquet, held in the steamer *Ida*'s saloon. Mr. Snyder was the first president of the Saugerties and New York Steamboat Company. To the extreme left in the second row is the captain of the *Ida*, Charles R. Tiffany. (Robert A. Snyder Collection.)

The *Ida*, purchased in 1904 to replace the *Saugerties*. *Ida* is seen here at Pier 43 in New York near Christopher Street. Like the other steamers, *Ida* burned coal to power its steam engines. The *Ida* was unusual in that it was an iron-hulled steamer. It was 200 feet in length and 55 feet in width. The *Ida*'s last sailing was in 1931. (Photograph by Ruth Reynolds Glunt, courtesy of the Saugerties Lighthouse Conservancy.)

The *Robert A. Snyder, c.* 1920. In 1920 the *Ulster* was overhauled and renamed *Robert A. Snyder.* The steamboats not only carried passengers, but carried freight as well. Goods, produce, and raw materials for the factories arrived in Saugerties. In turn, the Saugerties mills exported paper products to markets the world over. The steamboat era lasted over one hundred years, fostering tremendous economic and social development in Saugerties and the Hudson River Valley. (Courtesy of Kathleen and Edward Van Gaasbeek.)

Robert A. Snyder, c. 1936. River ice gouged a hole in the *Robert A. Snyder* in February of 1936, causing it to sink to the bottom of the Esopus Creek. On November 21, 1938, the *Robert A. Snyder* was towed out of the Esopus Creek, salvageable parts were removed at Staten Island, and the remainder of the hull was sunk in the Atlantic Ocean. (Hudson River Maritime Museum Collection.)

The *Air Line* ferryboat, Esopus Creek, *c.* 1875. Ferries transported people, wagons, and freight across the Hudson River. The *Air Line* ran for nearly sixty years between Saugerties and Tivoli. At Tivoli, connections to railroads or other steamboats could be made. Built in 1857 for the Air Line Railroad of Philadelphia, it started service on the Hudson in 1860. The *Air Line* was retired in 1915. (Photograph by Edward Jernegan from *The Pearl*.)

Remnants of the Saugerties Long Dock on the Hudson River, 1939. The Long Dock allowed for fast and convenient steamboat stops and also contained a terminal for eating and waiting and a warehouse for receiving freight. *The Saugerties Daily Post* of June 5, 1877, reported that Saugerties was "opened to the world" upon the construction of this landing. Over twelve hundred people attended the gala opening to welcome the steamers *Vibbard* and *Drew* to the Long Dock. (Saugerties Town Historian.)

The *Herman Livingston*, *c*. 1910. The *Livingston* connected Saugerties to the city of Hudson and other river towns. It made two trips a day, the first in the early morning and the second in the afternoon. Captain Winans owned the boat and began sailing in 1887. (Connie Lynch Collection.)

The *Saugerties* ferry, 1930s. Owned by the Hennay brothers, the ferry left from the Long Dock in Saugerties and made its trip across the Hudson River to Tivoli in about two minutes. The fare for a car and driver in 1938 was 40¢. Both the bow and the stern were open for quick loading and unloading. This was Saugerties' last operating ferry. (Saugerties Town Historian.)

Saugerties Rowing Club, 1875. The Saugerties Rowing Club on the upper Esopus Creek was organized in 1875. The boathouse was built at the mouth of the Tannery Creek, better known as the Muddy. The clubhouse had dressing rooms. Atop the building was a cupola. South of the boathouse was a course of 1.5 miles for shell-boat racing. (Connie Lynch Collection.)

Boaters on the upper Esopus Creek, c. 1910. The upper creek provided quiet waters for boating and fishing. Rowboats could be rented at Knight's Boat Rental near Beach Street in the village. (Saugerties Public Library.)

Dr. Robert E. Funk (right), state archaeologist of New York, and students, excavating at the Rocky Point Site in 1963. The site was located on the north side of the juncture of the Esopus Creek and the Hudson River. The artifacts indicated occupations from the Archaic Period (before 2000 B.C.) to the Middle Woodland Period (c. 800 A.D.). The occupants ate freshwater clams as indicated by the presence of shell middens. (Photograph by Ruth Reynolds Glunt, courtesy of Library Research Associates.)

Dolphin beached at Malden, 1930s. This dolphin met with a tragic end when it wandered too far up the river. The Hudson River, sometimes referred to as "The Arm of the Sea," is an estuary from its mouth to the dam at Troy. The river is tidal and contains salt until it reaches Poughkeepsie. Blue crabs, striped bass, and sturgeon are some of the saltwater creatures that inhabit sections of the river. (Connie Lynch Collection.)

Fishermen Frank Whitehead and his father, 1947. Hudson River fishermen used small boats when netting shad. In this case, one person rowed while the other pulled in the net. Frank Whitehead stood in the cuddey box that held the net and fish. Drift gill nets extended hundreds of feet across the river. The shad run occurs in the spring, and the fish average 5 pounds each. The shad roe is considered a delicacy. (From *The Sawyer*, 1947.)

Buoy motorboat, Esopus Creek, 1978. The United States Coast Guard tends the buoys and lighted towers on the Hudson River. This buoy motorboat has a forward boom that can lift up to 4,000 pounds. Buoys can be lifted out of the water and stored on the deck for repair or placement. In 1967, Coast Guard Aids to Navigation Team-Saugerties (ANT) started operation on the Esopus Creek. A previous United States Coast Guard Station was located at Turkey Point, 4 miles south of Esopus Creek harbor. (Courtesy of USCG ANT Saugerties, New York.)

Two
The Village

Main Street, 1905. Main Street was the center of activity in Saugerties. Bicycles were used by adults to zip around the village before cars became popular. Buggies traveled over the dirt streets, taking passengers to the numerous shops for merchandise, like clothing, hardware, and food. Main Street was a social and entertainment center where people attended theaters and gathered in saloons and restaurants. There were plenty of hotels and boardinghouses for summer tourists and visitors from rural areas who came to town for business or entertainment. Parades and celebrations usually took place along Main Street. The telegraph and post offices were there along with government offices and banks. Most of the commercial buildings on Main Street were constructed in the last half of the nineteenth century. This is a view from Market Street looking east. (Photograph by Lionel DeLisser from *Picturesque Ulster*.)

Main Street, south side, 1875. Horse-drawn sleighs were needed to travel over the packed snow in wintertime. The sign on the three-story building advertises Merritt's Dry Goods and Carpet Store. (Photograph by Edward Jernegan from *The Pearl*.)

Ox-drawn wagon, Main Street, *c.* 1905. Ox-drawn wagons were once a familiar sight in the village and the town. Oxen were cheaper, steadier, and more patient than horses. They were used to plow the fields, pull loads of logs and firewood, and were hitched to most wagons. (Saugerties Town Historian.)

Partition Street, east side, 1875. Advertising signs often extended over the sidewalk, including the signs for the John Kleeber Boot and Shoe Store and the tobacco shop. The trunks of the young trees along the street were encased in protective wood enclosures to prevent waiting horses from gnawing on the bark. (Photograph by Edward Jernegan from *The Pearl*.)

The Seamon Building on Main Street, built in 1882. The Seamon Brothers Company, established in 1873, sold furniture. The Seamon brothers were also funeral directors. A chapel, special rooms, and a morgue with a "lady in attendance" were housed in the building. Architect John A. Wood designed the building. A prominent architect in the Hudson Valley, Wood also designed the Kingston and the Newburgh armories and was involved in the planning of the Bardavon Theater in Poughkeepsie. (From "Official Souvenir Program: Old Home Week," 1911.)

Covered bridge over the Esopus Creek, c. 1874. Located just above the falls, the bridge was built in 1840 by Ralph Bigelow for Henry Barclay at a cost of $7,000. Known as a Burr Arch bridge (named after inventor Theodore Burr), it may have been the longest of this type in New York State, extending 262 feet. It remained a toll bridge until the early 1850s. In 1851 it was sold to the town for $3,000 and was made toll-free. (Photograph by Edward Jernegan from *The Pearl.*)

Bridge over the Esopus Creek, 1875. Located just above the dam and completed on December 30, 1874, the bridge was a wrought-iron, diagonal lattice, or truss, bridge. It was erected by Leighton and Hilt of Rochester. The bridge was 268 feet long and could hold 1,800 pounds per lineal foot. The cost of the bridge was about $25,500. (Photograph by Edward Jernegan from *The Pearl.*)

24

The A.C. Spatz Bottling Works, Cross Street. Established in 1888, the Spatz company bottled sparkling mineral waters in a variety of flavors. Deliveries were made to all parts of the Catskill Mountains using horse and wagon. In 1911 the company also marketed vanilla and lemon extracts, laundry blue, and household ammonia. Frederick W. Schneider was the proprietor at that time. (Courtesy of Harold Swart.)

Quick Brothers and Company Blacksmithing Shop, located on the corner of Livingston and First Streets, owned by E.L. and G.W. Quick and Andrew Jacobs. The shop was on the first floor and provided horseshoeing and repairing of all kinds at short notice. Wagons were made to order of any style or size. John A. Lowther, carriage and sleigh builder, had a shop over the Quick Brothers and Company c. 1898. (Courtesy of William and Vera Jacobs.)

The Old Brick Church Carriage House on Livingston Street, c. 1875. This carriage manufacturing and blacksmith shop was operated by George Burhans in the 1860s and 1870s. The structure was originally built as the first Reformed church in the village in 1827 under the leadership of Reverend Henry Ostrander. Services were held there for twenty-five years before the congregation outgrew its quarters. The building also served as the Saugerties Academy and the town hall. (Photograph by Edward Jernegan from *The Pearl*.)

The M.E. Donlon Store, c. 1915. Michael E. Donlon sold flour, feed, and groceries at his store on Ulster Avenue. The store was established in 1895 and was located just east of the West Shore Railroad Station. Mr. Donlon also sold insurance and was a notary public, according to a sign in front of the store. The owner, members of his family, and the store clerks are shown. (Courtesy of Harold Swart.)

A. Rightmyer Apothecary, on Market and Main Streets, *c.* 1886. This building was home to the C.L. Van Deusen Drug Store in the 1870s. It was known as Luther Hommel's Corner Pharmacy in 1911 and was advertised as being modern, legitimate, and scientific. The pharmacy was subsequently operated by John Martin, Charles Hauck, and Kenneth Beadle. The building was eventually torn down. (Courtesy of Harold Swart.)

John Kleeber Boot and Shoe Store, 120 Partition Street. Mr. Kleeber sold and repaired boots and shoes, and he re-leathered soles. Hats and caps were also sold there. The store opened *c.* 1875 and was still in operation in 1898. (Courtesy of Kathleen and Edward Van Gaasbeek.)

The E.M. Wilbur Store, located on Partition Street. The store was established in 1879 by E.M. Wilbur, who sold groceries and crockery. This photograph, taken in 1910, shows, from left to right, John Lowther, Mr. Butzel, Charles Wilbur, and Everett Rightmyer. (Courtesy of Harry McCarthy.)

E.M. Wilbur Store, interior. Kellogg's cereal, Campbell's beans, and Ball canning equipment were among the specialties sold at the E.M. Wilbur Store. Mr. Wilbur is shown in the center. (Courtesy of Harry McCarthy.)

Thomas J. Barritt's stationery store, corner of Main and James Streets, c. 1885. Mr. Barritt sold boxed paper, school supplies, stationery, books, and newspapers. His son, Leon Barritt, was a co-editor with Edward Jernegan of the magazine *The Pearl*. This monthly magazine had twelve issues covering topics of local interest during the year 1875. (Courtesy of Harry McCarthy.)

P.C. Smith's Hardware Store, Main Street. Philip Christian Smith worked as a tinsmith before purchasing the store in the late 1800s. The "Home of 10,000 Products" sold stoves, ranges, hardware, and metal ceilings such as the one seen here. (Courtesy of the Smith family.)

John C. Davis & Co. shoe store, corner of Partition and Main Streets, *c.* 1900. Established in 1846 by John W. Davis, father of John C. Davis, the store had two floors of stock that included boots, shoes, and straw hats. (Saugerties Town Historian.)

Candyland, Main Street, *c.* 1920. This confectionery store was loaded with homemade candy, much of which sold for a penny a piece. Homemade ice cream "made with 22% butterfat" could also be purchased. From left to right are Louis Chorvas, owner Stephen Chorvas, and an unidentified employee. (Courtesy of Michael Maclary.)

The Takas Store, Main Street, 1917–18. Dimitrios A. Takas (right) and Steve Stycos (left) posed in front of the tailor shop that Mr. Takas opened between 1905 and 1910. By 1912 the shop was well established and prospering. A shoeshine could be had for 5¢. Both men were born in Greece. They came to this country uneducated and penniless. Knowledge of their trade and hard work enabled them to realize the American Dream. (Photograph by George Jopson, courtesy of Andrew Takas.)

A young girl who was a living advertisement for Suderley's Bakery. Baked goods were tied to her dress, and she wore a hat made of bread. The Suderley Baking and Confectionery Company were wholesale jobbers in yeast cakes and baking powder. They were agents for Schraffts famous chocolates and for the National Biscuit Company. Suderley's Bakery was located on Partition Street. (Saugerties Public Library.)

Suderley's Bakery wagon, c. 1910. This horse and canopied wagon were used to deliver Blue Banner Bread, cakes, and pies to area boardinghouses and local residents. Suderley's Bakery was located at 95 Partition Street. (Saugerties Public Library.)

Paving Main Street. A line of bricklayers stretched across Main Street near the corner of Partition Street. Some of the workers were John Henry Kerbert, Frank M. Hughes, Connie Lynch, George Kerbert, Len Freligh, and G. Mills. (Courtesy of Frank Hughes.)

William D. Jacobs, *c.* 1920. Mr. Jacobs delivered Astor Tea and Coffee, pure extracts, and spices to area boardinghouses. (Courtesy of Vera and William Jacobs.)

Saugerties West Shore Railroad Station, west side of the railroad tracks on Ulster Avenue, c. 1909. Built in 1883, it served people going south to Weehauken, New Jersey, and north to Albany with connections for points beyond. This photograph of the passenger station shows Dick Van Buskirk's horse-drawn taxi waiting for customers. In the early 1960s, the station was torn down. (Courtesy of John Bubb.)

The West Shore Railroad Station, Ulster Avenue. The station was the scene of this "whistle-stop" speech c. 1912. Men made up the majority of the group gathered. They may have been "recruited" for the occasion. The speaker's identity is not known, but this event may have been a campaign speech by William Sulzer, who was elected governor with the strong support of labor that year. (Courtesy Mrs. Sharon R. Wilcox.)

The Exchange Hotel, Saugerties, N. Y.

The Exchange Hotel on Main Street, 1905. One of Saugerties' oldest inns, the Exchange was founded before 1848. A horse-drawn taxi stopped at the hotel to carry guests to the railroad station or the riverfront docks. In 1911 Charles H. Bennett was the proprietor. The hotel featured the American Plan at $2 per day. A garage and horse stables were in the rear. (Courtesy of Kathleen and Edward Van Gaasbeek.)

The Crystal House Hotel, *c.* 1908. Located at the junction of Hill and East Bridge Streets, Crystal House was a popular resort hotel. Summer guests posed on the porch for this postcard. James Reynolds, known for serving fine wines, liquors, and cigars, was proprietor in 1911. (Courtesy of Scherrell S. Schaefer.)

The Maxwell House Hotel, 1930s. The hotel and restaurant at the corner of Partition and Russell Streets was promoted as the leading hotel in town. An ad read: "located in the heart of the village . . . five minutes from the famous Esopus Creek, ten minutes from the station . . . electric lights . . . rates: $2.00 per day." (Courtesy of Scherrell S. Schaefer.)

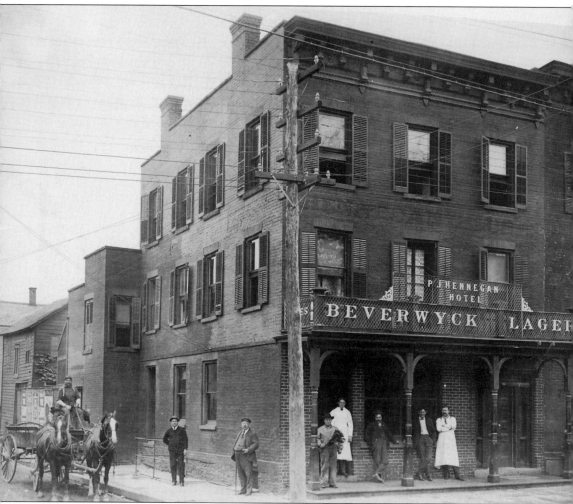

P.J. Hennegan House, Partition and Jane Streets, *c.* 1908. The proprietor, Peter Hennegan, advertised: "meals at all hours, including lunch; waiting rooms, and host boarders by day or week." Beverwyck Lager, made in Albany, was served on draught. Stables were attached to the rear of the building. Numerous hotels in Saugerties accommodated the tourists who frequented the area in the summer months. (Connie Lynch Collection.)

The South Side Hotel at the foot of West Bridge Street near the ferry line and the New York steamboat landings. The proprietor was Christy Hubert. (Courtesy of Scherrell S. Schaefer.)

South Side Hotel, East Bridge Street, 1910. Proprietor Christy Hubert, standing on the right, wisely located his establishment near the steamboat landings. He served a dinner to this party of gentlemen that included wine and a shellfish appetizer. The restaurant specialized in German cuisine. (Photograph by Fred Clarke from the Connie Lynch Collection.)

Children's Fountain, corner of Main and Market Streets, 1908. This fountain with lion-head spouts was constructed after local children raised money to build it. The fountain, which no longer stands, served as a drinking trough for horses. (Courtesy of Scherrell S. Schaefer.)

Dam on the Esopus Creek, 1902. A succession of dams at this site furnished waterpower to Saugerties' industries after Henry Barclay constructed his dam here in 1827. High water and ice constantly threatened the dams. The old wooden dam partially collapsed in 1902, but it was quickly repaired. (Courtesy of Kathleen and Edward Van Gaasbeek.)

Peter Campanelli, also known as Petey. Campanelli served as street cleaner in the village from the 1920s through the 1940s. Petey's cart, a metal can on large iron wheels, and other tools of his trade, a broom and shovel, were familiar sights from early spring to late fall. Petey's most remembered contribution to the community was his cheerful disposition. He was often referred to as "Saugerties' Ambassador of Good Will." (Courtesy of Kathleen and Edward Van Gaasbeek.)

Parade, Main Street. The parade participants were marching east on Main Street. The Exchange Hotel, on the right, was renting rooms for $1 per night. Cars were parked diagonally on the south side of the street. That custom continued until parking meters were installed. (Courtesy of Harold Swart.)

The Blizzard of 1888, still the benchmark by which all other winter storms are measured. From March 11 to March 14, the powerful storm battered the northeastern United States with an unprecedented combination of high winds, heavy snow, and cold temperatures. Winds whipped the snow into massive drifts. Snow was piled up to the roof of the historic Schoonmaker home (built c. 1727) at the east end of Main Street. (Courtesy of Elaine and Albert Genthner.)

The Washburn House, Washburn Terrace, 1905. The home of George W. Washburn was built in 1873 on the banks of the Esopus Creek at Stony Point. As the town and village prospered in the nineteenth century, large Victorian homes were built reflecting the wealth of local industrialists. The property was previously used as a public common known as the Clarkson Grounds. (Photograph by Lionel DeLisser from *Picturesque Ulster*.)

Saugerties High School, Main Street. The school was built in 1907 to accommodate the growing population of Saugerties. It was seen as a major step towards modernization and improvement in education for the Saugerties children. The building was converted to an elementary school in 1958, when a new high school was opened on Washington Avenue.

Students at the Livingston Street School posing for their yearly picture in 1887. The teacher was Mr. Cassells. (Courtesy of Harold Swart.)

The Saugerties Public Library, located on Washington Avenue, dedicated in 1915. The directors were Charles Clum, William S. Myer, and William Ziegler. The Andrew Carnegie Corporation contributed $12,500 towards the construction in 1914. Local Washburn brick and bluestone were used in the construction. The library houses a Moravian tile fireplace depicting the legend of Rip Van Winkle that was fashioned by American art tile maker Henry Chapman Mercer. (Courtesy of Scherrell S. Schaefer.)

The Ellen Russell Finger Home for Aged and Indigent Women, as it was originally known, located on the corner of Market Street and Ulster Avenue. In 1912 the house and some money were willed by Ellen Russell Finger for the purpose of sheltering women in need. In 1915 the home was incorporated, and a group of five trustees was appointed to manage it. In 1955 a board of management was set up to oversee the daily operation. In 1995 the facility closed. (Courtesy of Scherrell S. Schaefer.)

St. Mary of the Snow Roman Catholic Church, *c.* 1906. First known as the Parish of the Hudson, St. Mary of the Snow sits high on a knoll on the corner of Cedar and Post Streets. It was the first Catholic church between New York and Albany. Erected in 1833 under the leadership of Reverend Philip O'Reilly, the first parish served newly arrived Irish immigrants who worked in the iron, paper, powder mills, and the bluestone quarries. (Courtesy of Scherrell S. Schaefer.)

The original convent and school at St. Mary's of the Snow Parish. Built in 1879 as a rectory for the pastor, it became the Sisters of Charity Convent and school in 1881. According to local tradition, the three-story house was built, brick by brick, by men of the parish. Students from all classes are shown gathered on the front lawn for this photograph *c.* 1899. (Connie Lynch Collection.)

Trinity Church, Church Street, *c.* 1920. The church was incorporated in 1831. The establishment of the church and the building of the sanctuary were owed to the work of Henry Barclay, a nineteenth-century industrialist who donated the plot of land. A Sunday school was started in 1831, and within a year, 160 students were enrolled. In 1874 Mrs. Aaron Vanderpoel gave as a gift to the Episcopal church a memorial window by famed artist William Morris of London. (Courtesy of Scherrell S. Schaefer.)

The Saugerties Methodist Church, prior to 1918. The Methodist congregation was organized in 1829. Reverend S.L. Stillman was the first pastor. The structure on the right was used as the parsonage. A new church was built at the site in 1918. (Saugerties Public Library.)

The First Congregational Church, Main Street, 1870s. Organized in 1853, this was the first Congregational church in Ulster County. Reverend Smith B. Goodenow was installed as the first pastor. The steeple would eventually hold the historic town clock, manufactured by the A.F. Hotchkiss Company of New York and installed in the 1870s. The clock has four faces driven by a central mechanism. Over the years the clock has been maintained by the members of the church and financed by the village. (Courtesy of the First Congregational Church of Saugerties.)

Three
The Hamlets

Rural West Camp, *c.* 1890s. On the left is the Old Evesport Road, now known as Emerick Road, which gave access to the Hudson River. The road in the center that faces west toward the Catskill Mountains was the Old Evesport-Katsbaan Road, present-day Lauren Tice Road. In the late 1800s, the house in the center was known as the George Coons Hotel. In the 1920s, it was Hawley's Rooming House. (Courtesy of Ramona Sauer.)

St. Paul's Evangelical Lutheran Church, the oldest religious body in the town of Saugerties, located in the hamlet of West Camp. The congregation was organized in 1710 by Reverend Joshua Kocherthal and a group of German Lutheran Palatines. They had just arrived in the West Camp under an arrangement with Queen Anne which stated that the Palatines would work in the production of pitch, tar, rosin, and turpentine in return for passage to the colony. A similar contingent of Palatines settled on the opposite bank of the Hudson River. Reverend Kocherthal's church record book begins with a baptism performed aboard the ship *Globe* in 1708. Reverend Kocherthal's headstone is embedded in the wall of the narthex of the sanctuary. The present structure was built in 1871. (Courtesy of St. Paul's Evangelical Lutheran Church.)

Congregation of St. Paul's Evangelical Lutheran Church. Following World War II, between eight hundred and one thousand displaced persons (DPs) from the Baltic countries were brought to the United States under the sponsorship of Herman and Henry Knaust of Saugerties. The Knaust brothers employed most of the DPs in their mushroom-growing and canning industry. This 1951 group photograph at St. Paul's Evangelical Lutheran Church shows some of the DPs after they were received into the congregation. The Reverend Dr. Henry Schumann is shown on the left. (Courtesy of St. Paul's Evangelical Lutheran Church.)

West Camp, c. 1915. Looking north on old U.S. 9 West, this view shows a horse and wagon passing a motorcar on the dirt road. West Camp received its name in 1710, when the British government set up camps for the German Palatines on the west and east sides of the Hudson River. (Courtesy of Eleanor DeForest.)

The Katsbaan Reformed Dutch Church, located on Old King's Highway, as it appeared in 1855. The church was organized in 1730 by German Palatine emigrants of the Reformed faith. Temporarily, they shared worship facilities with the Lutherans at West Camp. The original stone edifice, erected in 1732, was changed somewhat through the years. The initials of some of the builders may be seen in the north wall of the building. (Photograph by Edward Jernegan from *The Pearl*.)

Cornelius Persen (1745–1827), owner of Persen's Store in the hamlet of Katsbaan. During the American Revolution, Persen brought merchandise from Philadelphia by an inland route because of the British occupation of New York City. Persen also made trips to Boston to purchase spices, tea, and salt. His store served as a meeting place for the patriots during the Revolution. Following the war, John Jacob Astor used the store for his periodic fur trading with local trappers. (Photograph from *The Early History of Saugerties*.)

The Trumpbour Homestead Farm, located on Old King's Highway in the hamlet of Asbury. The homestead, listed on the State and National Registers of Historic Places, is historically significant as a farm because it has been continuously occupied by a settlement period family beginning as early as 1732. The Trumpbour family's long farming occupation provides an important understanding of the settlement patterns of the West Camp German Palatine community. (Photograph by Karlyn Knaust Elia.)

Interior of Trumpbour Homestead, in the hamlet of Asbury. Around the fireplace of this eighteenth-century home are tools and utensils, including a flax wheel, candle molds, and whale oil lamp. (Photograph by Michael Saporito, courtesy of the Trumpbour Homestead.)

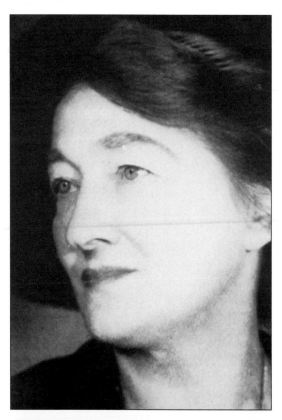

Dorothy Frooks, born and raised in the hamlet of Asbury. A lawyer and suffragist, she laid the groundwork for federal aid to dependent children and started the small claims court. She was a notable World War I navy recruiter and an enlistee herself. She founded the *Murray Hill News* and wrote for the *New York World*. Frooks attended her first school in Asbury, where her parents operated a summer boardinghouse. She died in 1997 at the age of one hundred. (Courtesy of Jay Vanderbilt.)

Trnka's Picnic Grounds and swimming hole, located in the hamlet of Asbury off of Wilhelm Road. The establishment, built by Fred Trnka in 1931, offered picnic facilities, a pavilion for dancing, a playing field, refreshments, and the cool waters of the Kaaterskill Creek for swimming. Trnka's was host to church and Sunday school picnics and also family and school gatherings. Fred Trnka sold the grounds in 1963. (Courtesy of Scherrell S. Schaefer.)

The Cliff House, Malden-on-Hudson, as it appeared c. 1918. The Greek Revival style house was originally built by the Isham family. It was later owned by John Maxwell of Malden, the bluestone magnate who earned nearly $1,000,000 in sales in 1875. The house was subsequently operated as a boardinghouse under the name Hover House and, later, as Cliff House. The house was eventually torn down. (Courtesy of Scherrell S. Schaefer.)

Stone docks, Malden-on-Hudson, 1875. Bluestone was brought to Malden to be cut to size, smoothed, and shipped. The two-story building in the center was the office of John Maxwell and the Bigelow Bluestone Company. Bluestone from Saugerties went to the growing urban centers of the nineteenth century. Large stones 15 feet long and 8 feet wide were used for city sidewalks. (From *The County Atlas of Ulster, New York*, 1875.)

John Bigelow (1817–1911), born and raised in the hamlet of Malden-on-Hudson. Bigelow graduated from Union College in 1835, and between 1848 and 1861, he shared ownership of the *New York Evening Post* with William Cullen Bryant. Bigelow accepted President Lincoln's appointment to serve the Union as U.S. Consul in Paris (1861–64) and was influential in preventing French assistance to the Confederacy. Bigelow published, in ten volumes, *The Complete Works of Benjamin Franklin (1887–88)* and was the chairman of the board of trustees that established the New York Public Library. Other Bigelow family members were also involved in the life and growth of Saugerties. (From *Retrospections of an Active Life*.)

Poultney Bigelow (1855–1954), known as the Sage of Malden, the son of John Bigelow. Graduating from Yale in 1879, he became active as an author and journalist. His writings covered a broad subject area, including travel observations, politics, and Colonial studies. He counted among his friends many politicians and world leaders. (Courtesy of Karlyn Knaust Elia.)

Portrait bust of Poultney Bigelow made by the sculptor Augusta Savage (1892–1962). Savage was a preeminent figure of the late Harlem Renaissance Period (1930s). Her life and work are currently undergoing a "renaissance" of re-discovery. Savage moved to Saugerties in the 1940s to live a quiet life. While in Saugerties, she worked in a local laboratory, participated in poetry readings, and remained active in art. The Bigelow bust was the last commissioned work by Savage and is dated 1951.

Francis Pidgeon House, 1875. This elegant home overlooking the Hudson River was built in 1867 one mile north of the village. Francis Pidgeon ran an industrial construction firm. He built dock facilities along the river and trestles for the West Shore Railroad. Later, George P. Hilton owned the home, and he remodeled it, calling it Stroomzeit. The building was destroyed by fire. (Photograph by Edward Jernegan from *The Pearl*.)

Pidgeon home interior. This image taken from a glass negative presents the finely appointed interior of the house. The women were elegantly adorned in Victorian period evening dress. (Courtesy of the Knaust family.)

The 60-foot tower on Mount Airy, in the hamlet of Quarryville. The tower is shown here as it appeared in 1875. Mount Airy is part of a chain of foothills known as the Hoogebergs. Built by Mr. Samuel Hommel, the tower provided panoramic views. (Photograph by Edward Jernegan from *The Pearl*.)

The Quarryville School, c. 1920. Built in 1849 on Blue Mountain Road in Quarryville, the building housed the pupils of the eight elementary grades. The school was arranged for two teachers. It was well supplied with educational equipment, according to an 1880 summary. The car near the school building belonged to Dick Emerick, the teacher at the time. The car proceeding down the road from Blue Mountain was owned by John Hennis. (Courtesy of Scherrell S. Schaefer.)

Franklin Delano Roosevelt, seated on the back seat of the convertible. Roosevelt is addressing a jubilant crowd at the Plattekill Reformed Church Fair in the hamlet of Mount Marion on July 5, 1937. President Roosevelt, the thirty-second president of the United States, who served from 1933 to 1945, was invited to the church by the Ladies Aid Society through the efforts of its president, Mrs. Warren D. Myer. (From the Franklin D. Roosevelt Library.)

The West Shore Railroad Station of the New York Central Railroad in Mount Marion, as it appeared c. 1910. Stops were also made in West Camp, Malden, and the Village of Saugerties. The railroad stations were built to standard architectural specifications, which accounts for the similarities in their designs. (Courtesy of Scherrell S. Schaefer.)

Christian Meyer Home, Mount Marion. Coming to West Camp with the Palatine emigration in 1710, Christian Meyer moved to "Churchland" west of Saugerties in 1724. He helped build the Katsbaan Church and inscribed his initials on the outside wall in 1732. Meyer owned three slaves in 1775, who worked on his farm. That year he also signed the Articles of Association, which supported independence from Britain. (Saugerties Historical Society.)

The Fish Creek covered bridge. The wooden bridge in the hamlet of Fish Creek stood over the Plattekill Creek near the site of a saw and gristmill. It was just upstream from the Laflin and Rand Powder Mill (1832–1874). The bridge, invented by Ithiel Town, was known as the Town Lattice Truss Bridge and was replaced by an iron bridge in 1901. (Saugerties Public Library.)

The Saugerties Reservoir, located in the hamlet of Blue Mountain. This 2.5-acre reservoir has a 12-million gallon capacity and is fed by numerous springs and three large streams: the Plattekill, the Lucaskill, and the Cotton. The privately-owned Saugerties Water Company built the original water system and operated it until 1896, when the village bought out the company. In 1926, major improvements were made, including completion of the dam, a chlorination facility, and an office. (Saugerties Public Library.)

The hamlet of West Saugerties, shown c. 1903. West Saugerties provided an approach to the Platte Clove and the majestic Catskill Mountains. Nineteenth-century artists such as Charles Lanman, Thomas Cole, and Frederick Church were inspired by its natural beauty. (Courtesy of Scherrell S. Schaefer.)

Hikers stopping to view the Lower Pearl Falls in the Platte Clove, 1875. The Catskill Mountains rise over 2,000 feet on either side of the clove. Numerous waterfalls varying from 5 to 100 feet in height provide the hiker with breathtaking rest stops. (Photograph by Edward Jernegan from *The Pearl*.)

Huckleberry pickers proudly displaying the day's harvest of sweet huckleberries. The fruit was gathered around the Platte Clove in the hamlet of West Saugerties. The succulent berries were made into jam and pies or added to muffins and pancakes. The berries that weren't used were sold to a local dealer. (From *Toodlum Tales*.)

OPUS 40. Harvey Fite purchased an abandoned bluestone quarry in High Woods in 1938. As he began placing his stone sculptures in the quarry, he decided to utilize the entire landscape. Using the ancient method of "dry keying," Fite needed no cement to hold the stones together. The title *OPUS 40* signified Fite's intention to work forty years on the project. Two years short of his target date, he died from a fall in the quarry at age seventy-three. (Photograph by Maria La Yacona, courtesy of *OPUS 40,* Inc.)

OPUS 40, a 6-acre environmental stonework created by sculptor Harvey Fite. Stone ramps and stairs connect different levels of curving terraces positioned against the backdrop of the Catskill Mountains. At the center stands an uncut, 9-ton monolith of bluestone. (Photograph by Robert Cline, courtesy of *OPUS 40,* Inc.)

Ladies Aid Society of the High Woods Reformed Church, 1963. The quilters were working in the old High Woods Schoolhouse when they made the "School House Quilt." Etta Wolven worked on the loom in the background. Seated around the quilting frame from left to right were Myrtle Shortt, Nita Gardner, David Wolven, Dora Felten, Emma Wolven, and Lynn Wolven. (Photograph by Charles Bryson, courtesy of the Saugerties Public Library.)

John Wolven home, Fred Short Road, High Woods, c. 1892. The Wolvens did subsistence farming, raising a variety of animals and crops for their own use. Horses did the heavy work. Even the dog ran a treadmill attached to a butter churn. The Wolvens fashioned linen clothes from flax they grew on their farm. From left to right are Alexander Wolven, Josephine Van Aken Wolven, and their children: Arthur, Lillian, Emma, Alice, and Uriah. (Courtesy of Francis Wolven.)

The Mountain View store, in the hamlet of High Woods, as it appeared in 1922. Henry Wilgus, owner, sold ice cream, beer, and general store merchandise. Since this building was also his home, he erected a new store and dance hall next door. It was for a long time the hub of the community, until it closed in the 1960s. (Courtesy of Vernon A. Benjamin.)

High Woods Reformed Church Sunday School students and teachers. The group must have enjoyed this outing with horse-drawn floats. Although the date and occasion are not known, floats were always expected in the parade that represented the climax of the church's annual Labor Day fair, begun in 1892. (Courtesy of Kathleen and Edward Van Gaasbeek.)

Cedar Grove School, 1959. Students in rural, one-room schoolhouses had one teacher for all subjects. The Cedar Grove School housed grades one through six and was one of the last of the old schoolhouses to close. (From *The Sawyer*, 1959.)

The Ernest Williams Summer Music Camp in the hamlet of Pine Grove, which operated from 1931 to 1947. Ernest Williams (1881–1947) played solo trumpet for the Philadelphia Orchestra under Leopold Stokowski, taught at the Julliard School of Music, and worked as a conductor. In 1931 he began holding summer music sessions in Saugerties. For sixteen years his camp thrived with a faculty that included renowned American composers and musicians. The camp closed in 1948. (From *Ulster Magazine*.)

Wooden covered bridge spanning the Esopus Creek in the hamlet of Glenerie near the Pleasant Valley Inn. Workers used horse-drawn wagons to haul materials needed to work on abutments for an iron bridge that was to replace the covered bridge. (Courtesy of Karlyn Knaust Elia.)

Pleasant Valley Inn (PVI), Route 9W and Glasco Turnpike, c. 1911. The hotel was a popular summer resort on the east bank of the Esopus Creek. Boating, bathing, and fishing activities were provided free of charge to guests. A livery stable was connected to the hotel. John Sauer was the proprietor. (Courtesy of Scherrell S. Schaefer.)

Saint Joseph's Church and the Fireman's Hall, Glasco, c. 1930. St. Joseph's became a parish in 1919. Reverend Henry Newey was the pastor. Many of the parishioners were Italians who worked at the brickyards. Fireman's Hall, built in 1900, was home to the Mulford Engine Company and the Washburn Hook and Ladder Company. (Courtesy of Scherrell S. Schaefer.)

The Washburn Store, located in the hamlet of Glasco and opened in the 1880s. The store was operated by the Washburn Brothers Company Brick Yard. The company store often carried brickyard employees' accounts on credit. The Washburn Brothers Brick Company was the immediate area's largest employer and encouraged European immigrants to settle in Glasco. Glasco got its name from a glass company's sign on a riverfront warehouse, which read "Glass Co." (Courtesy of Kathleen and Edward Van Gaasbeek.)

Schoentag's Hotel, Route 9W, Glasco, c. 1935. Schoentag's was a popular resort near the Esopus Creek. Tourists enjoyed bathing, boating, and fishing. Constructed c. 1825, the building became Martin's Inn in 1830. A post office was located there, and the building was used for elections. In 1911, it was called Glenerie Falls Hotel and had a bowling alley, a pavilion, and picnic grounds. (Courtesy of Scherrell S. Schaefer.)

Firefighters, Glasco, *c.* 1900. The Mulford Engine Company and the Washburn Hook and Ladder Company shared the firehouse in Glasco. The firefighters protected the community and the industrial complex on the Hudson River where the large wooden buildings for the brickyards and icehouses were located. (Connie Lynch Collection.)

Glasco Four Corners at the intersection of Glasco Turnpike and Route 32, *c.* 1930. Fuller's store, on the left, sold groceries and gasoline. (Courtesy of Helen and Charles Mayone.)

The Veteran Schoolhouse, located in the hamlet of Veteran (also called Toodlum and Unionville), built of bluestone in 1837. This photograph of the Veteran student body was taken in 1931. The teacher on the right was Mr. Paul Newkirk. (Courtesy of Shirley Hunter.)

Veteran Hotel, prior to 1922. William Crotty, on left and pictured here with Ed Ricks, ran this roadhouse and summer resort. It had a saloon frequented by many teamsters who drove loads of bluestone and wood to the village. Veteran was named by its first postmaster, Robert Sickler, a veteran of the Civil War. (From *Toodlum Tales*.)

Four
Industry and Commerce

Ulster Iron Works, *c.* 1830s. Built in 1828 by industrialist Henry Barclay (1778–1851) on the lower Esopus Creek, the Ulster Iron Works was one of the first industries in Saugerties. Barclay purchased land and secured extensive water privileges along the creek. He had a dam erected and cut a raceway through several hundred feet of rock to provide waterpower for the iron production. The Ulster Iron Works closed in 1888. In the background appears the lead mill, owned by Charles Ripley. The lead mill manufactured Minie rifle balls for use during the Civil War. (Courtesy of Inez and Charles Steele.)

John Simmons (1799–1878). Simmons became the first manager of the Ulster Iron Works on April 8, 1828, when he entered into a contract with the company for $700 per year. Mr. Simmons developed his knowledge of ironwork in his native England and in France. He was an originator of the "Double Puddling-Furnace." The Ulster Iron Works was possibly the first place in America where the "puddling" process of making iron was used. Molten iron was stirred by workers with paddles to separate the metal from impurities. In 1863 Mr. Simmons's connection with the iron mill ceased. (Courtesy of Evelyn Sidman Wachter.)

Replica of the original Terwilliger Mill, c. 1980. Terwilliger Mill, adjacent to Seamon Park, operated as a gristmill until 1910. There has been a mill at this site since before the American Revolution. Many other saw and gristmills were located on local streams and the Esopus Creek. In 1966 Mrs. Katharine Knaust gifted the mill site to the Village of Saugerties. In 1971 the Little Sawyer Association formed to create a replica, but the project was never completed. Still it is a reminder of the millers and sawyers of long ago and their importance to the growth of Saugerties. (Photograph by Michael Saporito.)

The J.B. Sheffield & Son's Paper Mill, 1875. Located on the south side of the lower Esopus Creek, the paper mill was started by Henry Barclay in 1827. In 1867 Sheffield became sole owner of the mill. The mill produced 1,000 tons of high quality paper per year using 4 tons of linen and cotton rags daily. The operation ran night and day and employed 150 people. In 1890, eleven years after the death of Joseph B. Sheffield, the company closed. (Photo by Edward Jernegan from *The Pearl*.)

The Pulp Mill, lower Esopus Creek. This building complex was home to the Ulster Iron Works until the iron works were shut down and sold to W.R. Sheffield in 1886. In 1888 Sheffield operated his pulp mill within the former iron works, and it closed in 1896. (Connie Lynch Collection.)

Ulster White Lead Company, Glenerie, *c.* 1890s. Colonel Edward Clark founded the lead company in 1835 to produce "white lead." Lead was formed into discs and filled with a water-vinegar solution. The discs were allowed to corrode and then were ground by water-powered machinery. The lead powder would later be added to paints. A community sprang up around the lead company, including a chapel, company store, and several homes. In the early twentieth century, the village fell to ruin. (Courtesy of Karlyn Knaust Elia.)

Workers at the Ulster White Lead Company, Glenerie, 1890. The company was nicknamed the "slow kill" due to the deleterious effects of the lead on the workers. The company closed *c.* 1900. (Courtesy of Kathleen and Edward Van Gaasbeek.)

The Ditch Quarry in the hamlet of Quarryville, one of the busiest producers of bluestone at the turn of the century. Most of the stone was taken to the Bigelow bluestone yards in the hamlet of Malden-on-Hudson for final preparation and shipping by barge. (Saugerties Town Historian.)

The Malden dock area on the Hudson River, a bustling spot in the 1890s. On the left, a ten-horse team is hauling a load of bluestone taken out of quarries in Quarryville. Convoys of wagons from various quarries hauled immense slabs of bluestone, some weighing as much as 18 tons, to the docks in Malden, Glasco, and along the lower Esopus Creek. On the right is the office of the Bigelow Bluestone Company and Malden telegraph office. (Saugerties Town Historian.)

Bluestone yard workers in the hamlet of Malden-on-Hudson. Between 1840 and 1850, sixty to one hundred loads of bluestone came to Malden daily from the hamlet of Quarryville. In 1875 the Maxwell Bluestone Co., successor to Bigelow, employed 125 men in the Malden yard. The men were employed as cutters and mill men who were to plane, axe, and finish the stone before transport. In 1873 approximately three thousand men and boys were engaged in quarrying in the town of Saugerties. (Courtesy of Don Curry.)

The Corner Quarry, or Carle and York Quarry, located in High Woods, shown between 1910 and 1915. Quarry workers are seen here using a large derrick to remove bluestone. Horses pulled the bluestone on wagons to the Burhans and Brainard Stoneyard and docks nearest the junction of the Esopus Creek and the Hudson River. The Corner Quarry closed c. 1917. (Courtesy of Francis Wolven.)

The Stone Dock, located on the north side of the Esopus Creek, shown in the foreground c. 1910. Here, bluestone from local quarries was delivered by horse and wagon for transport on the Hudson River. The steamships *Ulster* and *Ida* and the ferryboat *Airline* are shown in the background. (Connie Lynch Collection.)

Valley Farm, located just north of the village, c. 1900. Farming prospered in the fertile valleys surrounding the village. In 1875 Saugerties farms were producing dairy products, poultry, meat, pork, hay, seed, grain, maple syrup, grapes, apples, cider, wine, and livestock. In this photograph taken from a glass negative, horses are shown pulling a reaper. (Courtesy of the Knaust family.)

Stone lime kiln west of the Katsbaan Four Corners. This kiln was used to burn lime rock, which was used as fertilizer by local farmers and sold for 12¢ a bushel. By 1900, Nathan Fiero took over the business from his father, William. Four men were employed in the operation. The 40-by-40-foot kiln was demolished in 1927. (Courtesy of Joyce Fiero Tompkins.)

Ice harvesting on the Hudson River, Glasco, 1909. The natural ice industry flourished during the winter months when the Hudson River froze over and provided hundreds of men and boys from the farms, quarries, and brickyards with winter employment. The man on the left is Charles Mulford, who managed the Mulford Ice House in Glasco. (Saugerties Town Historian.)

Mulford Ice House, owned by the Knickerbocker Ice Company, Glasco. Each winter over 10,000 tons of ice were harvested here. When the icehouse was filled, hay was spread over the top of the ice to insulate it from the heat. A barge, tied to pilings, is shown being loaded with the frozen cargo. This immense icehouse was destroyed by fire in 1915, when a night watchman accidentally broke a kerosene lantern. (Connie Lynch Collection.)

The High Pond Ice Company and the Crystal Ice Company, Hill Street, c. 1893. Ice was harvested from the Esopus Creek and stored in large icehouses. Most of the ice from these companies was probably sold locally for use in homes, restaurants, and hotels. (From *Artwork of Ulster County*, 1893.)

The Little Sawyer Ice Company building at Valley Farm on the Sawyerkill, late 1920s. In this photograph, workmen are shown placing cakes of ice in a canal prior to loading them on the conveyor belt for storage in the icehouse. The implement on the right was used for scoring the ice to prepare it for the actual cutting. The ice company was owned by Martin Cantine, owner of the local paper coating mill. (Photograph by Ruth Reynolds Glunt, courtesy of Library Research Associates.)

Workers for the Little Sawyer Ice Company, located on the Sawyerkill. The workers are shown harvesting ice in the late 1920s. When the ice was frozen to 18 inches thick, harvesting would begin. First, if the ice was snow covered, the snow was scraped off using a horse-drawn snowplow (as shown). The ice was then scored, in grid fashion, into 2-inch strips. An iron plow did the final machine cutting, and men with long-handled tools made the last cut. The blocks were broken into individual cakes of ice. The cakes were then lifted on the conveyor belt into the icehouse for storage. Ice harvesting was made obsolete by refrigeration. (Photograph by Ruth Reynolds Glunt, courtesy of Library Research Associates.)

Martin Cantine (1866–1935), founder of the Martin Cantine Company, a manufacturer of coated paper. At seventeen, Cantine started working in the paper business as a salesman for the J.B. Sheffield Paper Company. In 1888 Cantine bought machinery from the Allston Adams Card Company of Albany for use in his mill on the Esopus Creek. (Courtesy of Nancy and Robert Moon.)

The Martin Cantine Company, 1898. The original one-story building measured 178 by 50 feet, and it contained a hand-cranked machine that handled 2 tons of coated paper per day. The company, founded in 1888 and located on Partition Street, harnessed waterpower from the dam on the Esopus Creek. (Courtesy of Kathleen and Edward Van Gaasbeek.)

Employees of the Martin Cantine Company, 1888. These were the first thirteen employees of the company. Located on lower Partition Street, the Martin Cantine Company manufactured coated paper. The high-quality papers were sold worldwide. Over the years the company grew and eventually employed four hundred workers. (Courtesy of Nancy and Robert Moon.)

Chain-drive truck owned by the Martin Cantine Company. Raw-stock paper would arrive at the train depot and be driven to the mill by the chain-drive truck. Coal, lumber, and clay (used in the coating process) arrived by boats on the Esopus Creek and were delivered to the mill by truck. Finished products were shipped out by the same methods. Pictured are Phillip Breithaupt (left) and Michael Kelly. (Courtesy of Kathleen and Edward Van Gaasbeek.)

Officers of the Martin Cantine Company, 1935. Holley R. Cantine (seated), son of founder Martin Cantine, began work at the mill in 1905. In 1935 he became president of the company. Standing, from left to right, are Lewis Fellows (treasurer) and Fred Fonda (secretary). (Courtesy of Nancy and Robert Moon.)

Workers in the Martin Cantine Company sorting room, c. 1930. The sorting room was well lit so that each sheet of coated paper could be properly inspected. Inspectors had two tables: one for perfect sheets and the other for rejects. Employees worked one year as helpers before becoming inspectors. (Courtesy of Nancy and Robert Moon.)

Martin Cantine Company, 1950. The Cantine Company flourished during the years following World War II. Over four hundred employees produced paper products requiring special processes that only Cantine performed. They made cartons for Old Gold cigarettes. After the mid-1950s, however, the business declined because the river was no longer an efficient avenue of transportation, pollution control equipment drained the company's funds, and competition from other paper companies cut Cantine's profits. (Photograph by Dick Smith.)

Fire at Cantine Mill, 1978. A devastating fire occurred at the Cantine factory on the afternoon of January 15, 1978. The fire spread through all the buildings of the complex. Over two hundred firefighters battled the flames in the cold weather and snow. Twenty fire companies responded. They managed to save nearby homes, but by morning the factory was in ruins. (Photograph by Dale Van Benschoten.)

Peter Canner Machine Company, corner of Livingston and Cross Streets, c. 1910. Peter Canner manufactured machinery used in Saugerties' growing brickyard industry, such as shafting, hangers, and pulleys. (Courtesy of Kathleen and Edward Van Gaasbeek.)

Staples Brickyard, located along the Hudson River in Malden-on-Hudson, as it appeared c. 1940. The brick industries in various parts of Saugerties were a major economic force from the late nineteenth century to the mid-twentieth century. (Courtesy of Helen W. Staples.)

Workers at the Staples Brickyard in Malden-on-Hudson. The employees are shown in 1953 inside a storage facility used for stacking clay molds. Staples Brickyard operated between 1910 and 1958 on 120 acres, using clay from the site. Staples Brickyard employed 125 people and shipped most of the brick by barge to New York City. Other brick companies in Saugerties included the Washburn Brothers Co., Lent, Doherty, Corse, and Empire. An earlier yard, probably the first in Saugerties, was near the end of Mower Mill Road in Cedar Grove. Oral history credits it as the source of brick for some early churches. (Courtesy of Michael Tagliaferro.)

General Douglas MacArthur (left), chairman of the board of directors of Sperry Rand Corporation, with Herman Knaust, president and founder of Iron Mountain Underground Security Vaults, October 21, 1952. Iron Mountain became the world's largest storage facility for microfilm. MacArthur and Knaust, standing behind a prototype of Iron Mountain, met to discuss a program to increase awareness of civil defense. Herman Knaust realized the need for a secure document storage facility after hearing accounts from war refugees of the total loss of their records during World War II. A son of German immigrants, Knaust was a lifelong resident of Saugerties. Because of his success in previous family business ventures within the community and beyond, he was able to develop the Iron Mountain project. He died in 1970 at the age of seventy-four. (Courtesy of the Knaust family.)

Knaust Brothers mushrooms, *c.* 1940. The "tray method" of growing mushrooms was developed and patented by Herman and Henry Knaust of Saugerties. The Knaust brothers began growing mushrooms in abandoned icehouses along the Hudson River. Their company prospered into the largest mushroom industry in the world, with nearly 15 million pounds grown annually. The Knaust brothers were leaders in mushroom canning, with 20 million cans bearing their "Cavern Brand" mushroom label produced annually. Salustiano Berzal was another major mushroom producer in Saugerties. (Courtesy of the Knaust family.)

The Saugerties Book Bindery building, East Bridge Street, constructed in *c.* 1888 and seen here in a photograph taken *c.* 1950. In this building the Saugerties Manufacturing Company, incorporated in 1895, produced loose-leaf binders and notebooks. They guaranteed overnight delivery of goods to New York City via the Hudson River. The company moved to Ulster Avenue in 1936 under the management of Fabian L. Russell. Other occupants of the building were Knaust Brothers Mushrooms, General Electric, Ferroxcube, and a chicken packing company. (Courtesy of Philips Corporation.)

Fabian L. Russell (1900–1979). Having been asked to help prevent the Saugerties Manufacturing Company from being liquidated, Russell moved from Holyoke, Massachusetts, to Saugerties several weeks before the Great Depression. He joined the company in 1929 and by 1943 changed its name to F.L. Russell Corporation; he was president of the company until 1969. Russell was known for his quiet acts of benevolence. (Courtesy of Mrs. Robert S. Russell.)

The F.L. Russell Corporation, located on Ulster Avenue. The company began operation at this site in 1936 after moving from their quarters on East Bridge Street. F.L. Russell produced the popular "composition" notebooks with the mottled black and white covers, loose-leaf binders, and photograph albums. Fabian L. Russell was president of the company until 1969, when his son, Robert S. Russell, succeeded him. In 1962 the company moved to a new location in Mount Marion. (From *The Sawyer*, 1950.)

Assembly line workers at the F.L. Russell Corporation, 1950. These workers are placing the wire binders on Sterling notebooks. (From *The Sawyer*, 1950.)

Thruway construction, 1950. The section of the New York State Thruway in Saugerties was called the Catskill Thruway. In the mid-twentieth century, there was a shift away from river and rail transportation to the highways. The thruway parallels the Hudson River-Erie Canal corridor that connects New York City to Buffalo. (New York State Archives.)

Five

Service

Washington Hook and Ladder Company, c. 1900. Organized in 1854, the Washington Hook and Ladder Company is one of Ulster County's oldest fire companies. Fireman's Hall in the background was located on Partition Street and built in 1873. The fire engines, hoses, and other equipment were stored on the ground floor, and the upper floors were used as quarters for the firefighters and as meeting rooms. The entire hall was destroyed by fire in 1939. The Saugerties Fire Department was established in 1834, and the Ladies' Auxiliary, in 1970. (Courtesy of Harold Swart.)

Ernest Hassinger, *c*. 1898. Ernest Hassinger served as chief of the Saugerties Fire Department. The trumpet under his arm acted as a megaphone so that the chief's orders could be heard. Hassinger collected fire-fighting memorabilia, especially badges depicting nineteenth-century firefighters and fire companies. Hassinger was in the business of making and selling fine cigars, and he participated in the Saugerties Bicycle Club and the Esopus Bathing Club. (Courtesy of Saugerties Exempt Firemen's Association.)

The Saugerties Exempt Firemen's Association, c. 1900. The members formed a line at the intersection of Partition and Main Streets. The term "exempt" signified that the firefighters were exempt from jury duty. That benefited firefighters in rural areas, because a trip to the county seat for jury duty would cost valuable days away from farm work. (Courtesy of the Saugerties Exempt Firemen's Association.)

Minnehaha, Partition Street, 1875. The fire department spent $4,000 in 1873 for this steam-driven pumper. The metallic cylinder to the left was the coal-burning steam engine. Before the fire hydrant system was built, the villagers used water-filled cisterns at various locations for fire-fighting. (Photograph by Edward Jernegan from *The Pearl*.)

The Saugerties Exempt Firemen's Association, 1900. The poster shows forty-one members with foreman D.N. Finger at the center. After five years of fire-fighting service, a member of any hose company could become an "exempt." Many leading members of the community were in the association. The Saugerties Exempt Firemen's Association was founded in 1892. (Courtesy of Harold Swart.)

Firefighters, 1916. Members of the Robert A. Snyder Hose Company enjoyed the camaraderie at a convention in Poughkeepsie. Identified by name but not position are Lyman Hallenbeck, Walter Hallenbeck, Fred Van Voorhis, William Ziegler, Charles Bridgman, A.D. York, Isadore Brown, and Louis Rovengo. (Courtesy of the Saugerties Exempt Firemen's Association.)

Robert A. Snyder Hose Company Band, 1911. Some fire companies formed their own band. This twenty-five-piece band was formed in 1905. Henry T. Keeney was president and Charles T. Sickles was vice president of the band in 1911. The Robert A. Snyder Hose Company No. 1, located on Partition Street, was formed in 1882. (From "Official Souvenir Program: Old Home Week," 1911.)

Colonel Theodore Burr Gates, in a c. 1863 photograph by Matthew Brady. Colonel Gates served with the 20th New York State Militia, which was composed of men from Ulster and Greene Counties during the Civil War. When Colonel George Watson Pratt was mortally wounded at the Second Battle of Bull Run in 1862, Gates replaced him as colonel of the 20th. The unit participated in battles at Antietam, Fredricksburg, and Gettysburg. At Gettysburg, Gates and his men helped repulse the Confederate Army's main assault, known as Pickett's Charge. From 1851 to 1853, Gates was co-editor of the *Saugerties Telegraph*, a local newspaper. After the war, he wrote a book entitled *The Ulster Guard and the War of the Rebellion*, which was published in 1879. (From the Seward R. Osborne Collection.)

Captain Walter Scott of Saugerties, Company G, 120th New York Volunteer Infantry, in a c. 1863 photograph taken by Bogardus. In July of 1862, President Lincoln called for three hundred thousand men to join the Union forces. By the end of August, many new regiments had formed, including the 120th. Most of the soldiers came from Ulster and Greene Counties. Of the eighty-nine men in the original company, twenty-five died during the war. Walter Scott died in Mexico in 1881. (From the Seward R. Osborne Collection.)

Captain Ira Swart of Saugerties, in a c. 1863 photograph taken by Edward Jenegan. Also answering President Lincoln's call, Ira Swart enlisted in August 1862 as a private in Company G. He rose steadily through the ranks. He was promoted to first sergeant at Gettysburg on the first day of the battle, July 1, 1863. He became captain of Company G, replacing Walter Scott in 1865. (From the Seward R. Osborne Collection.)

Ethan Wolven, c. 1863. Twenty-one-year-old Ethan Wolven of Saugerties joined the Union army in 1862. He was a private in Company G, 120th New York Volunteer Infantry. He posed, rifle in hand, for this tintype photograph. Photographic studios often sold tintypes mounted in leather cases with ornate metallic mats framing the pictures. (Courtesy of Kathleen and Edward Van Gaasbeek.)

Ulster County veterans' excursion to Devil's Den, Gettysburg, c. 1870. Civil War veterans from Saugerties joined this group of soldiers returning to the Gettysburg battlefield. Saugertiesians were members of the 20th and 120th regiments, which took part in the Battle of Gettysburg. This pivotal battle raged from July 1 to July 3, 1863. The Union victory shifted the tide of war in favor of the North. Over a thousand men from Saugerties participated in the Civil War. (Courtesy of Harold Swart.)

George Coons (1846–1932) of Saugerties, c. 1915. Mr.
Coons was a first-class seaman in the Union navy. He
served aboard the USS *North Carolina* in the United
States Navy Yard early in 1864. In December of that year,
he saw combat aboard the USS *Pawtuxet*, which attacked
Fort Fisher and Fort Anderson in North Carolina during
1864 and 1865. (Courtesy of Ramona Sauer.)

Civil War veterans in front of the Saugerties Bank,
c. 1915. Members of the Grand Army of the Republic, a
Civil War veterans' organization, participated in a parade
on Main Street. George Coons is sitting in the back seat
in the center. (Courtesy of Ramona Sauer.)

World War I soldiers, *c.* 1918. At Mountain View Cemetery, the soldiers paid homage to their fallen comrades on Memorial Day. The men, in full uniform, are, from left to right: (front row) Grant Brinnier, Gilbert Myer, Harold Farrell, George James, and Harry Carle; (middle row) Ernest Ackert, Edward Taylor, James Flanigan, Edgar Smith, Frank Martin, Ernest Sylvain, and Lyman Halenbeck; (back row) Les Mulford and unidentified. Over twenty Saugerties men perished in World War I. A plaque in front of the town hall on Main Street bears the inscription: "In honor of all those from the Town of Saugerties who served their country in the World War 1914–1918." The plaque was erected by the Saugerties Chapter of the Daughters of the American Revolution. (Courtesy of the Lamouree-Hackett Post No. 72 American Legion.)

World War II veterans. In 1944 and 1945, the Saugerties High School yearbook had collages picturing over two hundred local men and women who served during the war. Pictured here are the servicemen and women depicted on the last page of that collection: (bottom row) Irene Thornton, Franklin Auer, Ben Sanford, and George Swart; (second row) Wilson Van Vlierden, E.J. Myer, and Gus Hoffman; (third row) William and Dick Loerzel, Leslie Brooks, and George W. Sparling; (top row) Merril Garrison, Don and Wilbur Schaffer, and Warren Myer. (From *The Sawyer*, 1945.)

Colonel Roger H. Donlon, a native of Saugerties. Donlon was the first Congressional Medal of Honor recipient in the Vietnam War. Donlon was cited for his "conspicuous gallantry, extraordinary heroism, and intrepidity at the risk of his own life above and beyond the call of duty." This photograph, taken at the White House, shows President Lyndon B. Johnson pinning the Congressional Medal of Honor on Captain Donlon on December 5, 1964. (Courtesy of Paul Donlon.)

The Village of Saugerties Police Department with their new 1941 Dodge. From left to right are Edward Dillon, Chief Arthur Richter, Vernon Benjamin, John Keeley, William Rightmeyer, and Harold Mills. (Saugerties Town Historian.)

Six
Leisure Activities and Organizations

"Tom Thumb Wedding," 1941. A film crew from the Motion Picture Association of America produced the movie *Saugerties on Parade*. The original 35mm movie ran ninety minutes and was sponsored by local merchants. A segment of the film, the "Tom Thumb Wedding," was staged by Willett Overbaugh of Overbaugh's Florist. The mock wedding took place in the Reformed Church of Saugerties on Main Street. Pictured from left to right are Jim Gardner, Donald Lezette, Peter Banks, Jerry Gardner, Barbara Genthner, Joan Roosa, Nancy Tymeson, and John Sauer. Unfortunately, the original film was destroyed and no copies were made. (Courtesy of Millie and Willett Overbaugh.)

Lom Poo Base Ball Club, c. 1890s. Lom Poo was the first adult sports team to represent Saugerties. Organized in the late 1890s, this amateur baseball team was one of the many colorful organizations that made Saugerties a center of sporting activity over the years. The names of the players are, from left to right: (front row) Frank Sweeney, George Sief, and Enoch Whitney; (middle row) Peter Wilson, Martin Cantine, and Willis Pierce; (back row) William Peters, Charles Fellows, George Maines, and Emmett Crowley. (Connie Lynch Collection.)

Boys' basketball team, 1913. Principal and Superintendent Walter S. Smith posed with the boys' basketball team that had four wins and seven losses that year. At that time, a tip off followed every score. By controlling the tip offs, a team could dominate a game. Catskill did so that year, beating Saugerties 70–5. (From *The Sawyer*, 1913.)

Bicyclist gathering, hamlet of High Woods, 1890s. The cyclists are, from left to right, Annie Van Aken, Lena Carle, and Leah Margaret York. (Saugerties Public Library.)

Bicycle path, Glenerie, c. 1900. In 1899 bike riding was in vogue. Henry McName cleared a bicycle path from the Glenerie Falls Hotel going south. The path followed the tree-lined bank of the Esopus Creek. (Courtesy of Harold Swart.)

Saugerties members of the League of American Wheelmen, c. 1914, shown on an outing. Members included, from left to right, William Ziegler, Clyde Van Steenberg, Ed Snyder, Arthur Van Steenberg, Ben Davis, and Charles McCormick. The League of American Wheelmen campaigned for widespread road improvement and was the precursor of the Automobile Association of America. (Courtesy of Harold Swart.)

The first car in Saugerties, a 1904–05 Oldsmobile owned by Dr. Rudolf Diedling, who was a local physician. The car had tiller steering, wooden spoked wheels, kerosene lamps, and an 8 hp engine with one cylinder. It had a maximum speed of 30 miles per hour. Dr. Diedling appears with Alsen Cement Company officials and friends in Alsen, just north of Saugerties on Route 9W. In the car are Dr. Diedling (on the left) and Ed Snyder, and standing on the right, Lynn Bancroft. (Saugerties Historical Society.)

The Orpheum Theater, Main Street. J.C. Dawes built the theater in 1890. The Orpheum was used for vaudeville shows, movies, roller skating, and basketball. In 1920 Byron Thornton purchased the theater and began renovations to better accommodate motion pictures. A 50¢ ticket bought admission to four vaudeville acts and a feature film in 1921. Cary Grant, Joan Crawford, George Burns, and Gracie Allen made appearances on the Orpheum stage. (Saugerties Town Historian.)

Bijou Theater, Main Street, *c.* 1918. Shows included live singing and dancing acts. The brick building, with an elegant cast-iron facade, was built between 1885 and 1890. (Courtesy of Scherrell S. Schaefer.)

Queen Flo and her court, 1911. Queen Flo, who was crowned by Mayor Albert Rowe, of Saugerties, led the parade with her appointed maids of honor on Monday evening, July 3, 1911. Old Home Week celebration in Saugerties, held in conjunction with the Fourth of July celebration, was a well-planned, four-day event. Parades, carnivals, speeches, ballgames, fireworks displays, band concerts, and worship were all part of the program. (Courtesy of Shirley Hunter.)

Senior play at Saugerties High School, 1953. Only in a comedy about a bungling bandit would four crime victims look so happy. The play was *Nobody Sleeps*. The players are, from left to right, William Tongue, June Thornton, Shirley Vedder, Virginia Royael, and Patricia Fusick. (From *The Sawyer*, 1953.)

Parade of the Tri-County Firemen's Association, October 4, 1893. A large crowd of enthusiastic spectators turned out to watch a parade of fire companies. A hose company from Catskill marched up Partition Street. (Courtesy of Harold Swart.)

The Russell Block Building, corner of Main and Market Streets, 1893. The three-story brick building was festooned with stars and stripes on October 2, 1893, for the Firemen's Parade. This large commercial building housed the new post office and the Wesley Shultis Dry Goods store in 1898. The Shultis store sold groceries, crockery, glass, stoneware, fish, and corsets. The Russell Block Building was built in 1878. (Courtesy of Harry McCarthy.)

Parade float, 1921. The Evangelical Lutheran Church of the Atonement Sunday School class made a float out of flowers for the Fourth of July parade. The congregation was organized as the German Evangelical Lutheran Society of Saugerties in 1859. The church was erected in 1896. In 1914 the congregation adopted the name "The Evangelical Lutheran Church of the Atonement," and the German language was officially phased out. (Courtesy of Shirley Hunter.)

Parade on Main Street, July 1921. During Old Home Week, Saugertiesians and out-of-town guests celebrated Independence Day with a four-day festival. Parades, baseball games, band concerts, and fireworks thrilled the crowds. This picture shows the Floral Parade of Sunday Schools and Parochial Schools. (Courtesy of Harold Swart.)

Children with donkey, c. 1905. These village children were treated to a donkey ride. Richard Mullen is on the donkey, and brother Harold is standing. (Courtesy of Kathleen and Edward Van Gaasbeek.)

John J. Hayes Stone Works. These four men played a game of cards atop a piece of cut stone at the stone works on Ulster Avenue. In 1914 the establishment produced tombstones and took pride in "chiseling the most delicate outlines of a monument." From left to right are Henry Genthner, Orville Teetsel, John Hayes, and Edward Van Gaasbeek. (Courtesy of Kathleen and Edward Van Gaasbeek.).

Monday Club of Saugerties, 1932. The members of the Monday Club planted a tree at the Hill Street School to honor George Washington. The Monday Club was founded by Mrs. Howard Gillespy in 1896. This literary club was formed to promote benevolent projects and mutual improvement. The club was responsible for the formation of the Saugerties Cemetery Association. (Courtesy of Mrs. Robert S. Russell.)

International Order of Free and Accepted Masons, or Freemasons. The group, organized in 1848, was chartered under the name Ulster Lodge No. 193, F. & A.M. in 1850. The order's teachings promote integrity, good citizenship, and morality. Members in 1938 were, from left to right, (front row) Fred Eckerlein, Charles Wilbur, and Harold Winchell; (back row) Ralph Hayes, Kenneth Coons, Francis V. Reuther, Jacob Rogers, and William Bienn. (Courtesy of Harry McCarthy.)

Beach on the Hudson River, West Camp, c. 1905. On the shore of the Hudson River, swimmers cooled off on a summer day in bathing suits resembling full-length dresses. (Courtesy of Eleanor DeForest.)

Sailing on the Hudson River, 1945. Students from Saugerties High School took a leisurely sail on the Hudson and are seen returning to the Esopus Creek. Recreational sailing is a popular sport on the Hudson River. (From *The Sawyer*, 1950.)

Fishing derby at the Sawyerkill, 1958. The Saugerties Junior Chamber of Commerce sponsored a fishing derby for children. From left to right are Priscilla Stafford, Theodore Faulkner, Mr. Harold Hagopian (derby chairperson), Edmund Whitaker, Glen Stafford, and John Stafford. Priscilla won first prize with a 2-pound, 5-ounce carp. (Saugerties Town Historian.)

Fisherman, 1981. Sport and commercial fishing are common activities on the Hudson River. This boat was rigged with a scap net, normally 5 feet square, which is lowered into the water by a winch and quickly raised. Scap nets are used for catching carp, smelts, herring, and shad. Fisherman Joseph Lawless is shown in the boat. His family has been fishing the Hudson River since the 1890s. (Photograph by Michael Saporito, Saugerties Town Historian.)

Childrens Fountain,
Seamon Park, Saugerties N.Y.

Seamon Park, Malden Avenue. The park was presented to the Village of Saugerties by John Seamon in 1909 as a recreational park. Seamon wanted to create "a park, a breathing place, open and free at all times to every person." The park presents a magnificent view of the Catskill Mountains and of the village. Mr. Seamon expended a large sum of money in beautifying the property with its fountains and gardens. (Courtesy of Scherrell S. Schaefer.)

The Catskill Mountain House, c. 1910. The structure was an elegant Greek Revival style hotel perched between North and South Mountains to the northwest of Saugerties, with a view overlooking the Hudson River Valley. It was the scene for this happy gathering of young people from Saugerties. Some local people were employed at the hotel. (Courtesy of Harry McCarthy.)

118

Seven
Growing Gracefully

Saugerties as seen from across the Hudson River. The unique location of Saugerties has shaped the lives of its people. The Hudson River is one of America's great waterways. It provides fishing, recreation, and transportation. It links Saugerties to other parts of the Empire State, to New York City, and to the world. The Esopus Creek, a tributary of the Hudson River, is a safe harbor for ships and boats plying the Hudson. The waterfall on the Esopus Creek generated the power needed when the Industrial Revolution took hold in the Hudson Valley. Beyond the town, the scenic Catskill Mountains rise to the west; their natural beauty has long attracted visitors to Saugerties. (Photograph by Susannah Satten.)

The Saugerties Lighthouse. The Lighthouse Conservancy formed in 1985. The neglected structure of rotting wood and crumbling brick underwent repairs under the supervision of architect Alex Wade. The painstaking process of restoration continued until 1990, when the Saugerties Lighthouse was returned to operation and opened to the public. It adjoins the Ruth Reynolds Glunt Nature Conservancy, a natural preserve with a hiking trail to the lighthouse. (Photograph by Michael Saporito, courtesy of the Saugerties Lighthouse Conservancy.)

Clifford C. Steen and Jean Wrolsen at a gallery opening of Wrolsen's drawings, 1980. Under Steen's leadership, the downtown district was placed on the National Register of Historic Places in 1982. He spearheaded the restoration of the Saugerties Lighthouse through the Lighthouse Committee of the Saugerties Arts Council. Jean Wrolsen wrote a series of background articles on the fate of the lighthouse. For fifty years as an artist, poet, and journalist, Jean has focused on Saugerties. (Photograph by Dr. Richard Messina.)

Seamon Park, 1985. The park is the site of the annual Mum Festival that began in 1965, founded by Mr. William Voerg. Festival-goers enjoy the fall colors accented by the bright display of several thousand chrysanthemums. The festival includes music, crafts, and an art show, which occurs in October. Chrysanthemum means "golden flower." Mums are the earliest cultivated perennial on record, having been grown for over two thousand years. (Photograph by Dick Smith.)

The Hudson Valley Garlic Festival. Originated in 1989 by Pat Reppert, this festival is presented by the Kiwanis Club of Saugerties. Every September the aroma of garlic flavors the air. Upwards of forty-five thousand visitors savor garlic of many varieties. Everything imaginable is served with garlic flavor, from garlic bread to garlic snow cones. (Photograph by Mark McCarroll.)

Maurice D. Hinchey, born in 1938 and raised in Saugerties. Hinchey, a Democrat, was elected to the U.S. House of Representatives in 1992. He was reelected in 1994 and 1996. Hinchey's work in Congress has focused on the environment, banking and finance, and economic development. He wrote legislation that established the Hudson Valley as an American Heritage Area. While a member of the New York State Assembly (1975–1992), Maurice Hinchey wrote the act that created the Hudson Valley Greenway. As a state legislator, he sponsored the law that gave the Saugerties Lighthouse to the Saugerties Lighthouse Conservancy.

The *Clearwater*, a replica of the Hudson River sloops of old. The *Clearwater* was promoted by Vic Schwartz and folk singer Pete Seeger to raise public awareness of the Hudson River's history and environmental problems. Educational programs in sailing and ecology are conducted aboard the ship. The Connie Lynch Marina on lower Esopus Creek, in Saugerties, has long been the winter home of the *Clearwater*. (Photograph by Michael Saporito.)

Up for bid. In the 1980s antique stores began to flourish in Saugerties. Artwork, furniture, and vintage clothing were just some of the types of merchandise sold. Auctions are an important part of the antique scene. On the left is auctioneer Sheldon Siper, and on the right, displaying the merchandise for bid, is Donny Malone. (Photograph by Michael Saporito.)

The Philips Corporation at Saugerties, located off the New York State Thruway. The Ferroxcube Corporation started operations on East Bridge Street in 1950. The company built permanent magnets used in televisions. Ferroxcube became part of the Philips Corporation. The business moved in 1961 to the new site near the thruway. The company makes high-tech optical crystals and ceramics. (Courtesy of the Philips Corporation.)

Saugerties Dutchmen Base Ball Club, 1980. The team celebrated after the pennant-clinching win on July 27 (Tommy Whitaker is on the right). After an absence of two decades, adult baseball returned to Saugerties in 1980. The Dutchmen went on to become champions of the Hudson Valley Rookie League in 1980, their first season. The Dutchmen play at the well-equipped Cantine-Veterans Memorial Sports Complex. (Photograph by Michael Saporito.)

John Hall performing at the "No Nukes" concert at Madison Square Garden, 1979. Life in the Catskills has attracted many artists to Saugerties. Guitarist and vocalist with the band Orleans, John Hall's hits include "Dance with Me" and "Still the One." A political and environmental activist, Hall worked as an Ulster County legislator and a member of the Saugerties Central School Board.

Tomas Penning (1905–1982), artist. Tomas Penning discovered the adaptability of bluestone as a sculpting medium. His studio was in an abandoned stone quarry in High Woods. He often portrayed religious themes, as in "Our Lady of the Hudson," which overlooks the river at Port Ewen. She cradles a tugboat in her arms. (Courtesy of James Cox Gallery.)

Joe Sinnott, cartoon illustrator, 1962. In 1950 Joe Sinnott was hired by Stan Lee, the editor of Marvel Comics. He contributed to Marvel's successful revival of pre-war comic heroes Captain America and Submariner. Building on that, Marvel created more superheroes like the Incredible Hulk, Spiderman, the Mighty Thor, and the Fantastic Four. Sinnott also illustrated the Treasure Chest educational comic book series that included a biography of Pope John Paul II. He has resided in Saugerties all his life. (Photograph by Ronald B. Johnstone.)

Woodstock '94. All roads led to the Winston Farm in Saugerties for "3 More Days of Peace and Music" on August 12–14, 1994. It was the 25th anniversary celebration of the original Woodstock festival held in Bethel, New York, in 1969. The festival drew some 350,000 music fans. A varied mix of musical acts pleased both Generation X'ers and the more mature hippies of the 1960s generation. (Photograph by Michael Saporito.)

Woodstock '94. When the summer rains fell, the earth turned to mud. The going became slippery, but the "Mud People" sloshed in the slop in revelry. (Photograph by Michael Saporito.)

Let Saugerties Grow Gracefully mural, Market Street, 1990. The Winston Farm Alliance was formed in 1989 to respond to a decision to site a landfill in the heart of Saugerties. Over forty community organizations joined the Alliance. Community support ran high. This mural, designed by Saugerties artist F. Tor Gudmundsen and painted by Kate and Kurt Boyer, was a rallying place for the activists. Through public hearings, letter writing, demonstrations, and legal action, the plan to build the "mega-dump" was thwarted. Words to *The Saugerties Song* by John Hall are written at the base of the mural: "With the river flowing to the east, and the mountains rising in the west, we must provide for those who came before, those knocking at the door, and those yet to be born" (copyright 1988 by Siren Songs). (Photograph by Michael Saporito and courtesy of Allen Bryan.)

Bibliography

Anderson, Mark. "A High Note," *Ulster Magazine* (summer 1993): 61.

Artwork of Ulster County. Chicago: W.H. Parish Pub. Co., 1893.

Barritt, Leon and Edward Jernegan. *The Pearl*. Saugerties, NY: Barritt and Jernegan, 1875.

Beers, F.W. *County Atlas of Ulster, N.Y.* New York: Walker and Jewett, 1875.

Bigelow, John. *Retrospections of an Active Life*. 2 vols. New York: Baker and Taylor Co., 1909.

Bigelow, Poultney. *Seventy Summers*. New York and London, 1925.

Brink, Benjamin Myer. *The Early History of Saugerties, 1600–1825*. Kingston, NY: R.W. Anderson and Son, 1902.

Commemorative Biographical Record of Outstanding Citizens in Ulster County. Illinois: J.&H. Beers Co., 1896.

Frankel, Joseph and James R. Wood, eds. *The Saugerties Post: Special Edition*. (November 1898).

De Lisser, R. Lionel. *Picturesque Ulster*. Kingston, NY: Styles and Bruyn Pub. Co., 1896–1905.

Frooks, Dorothy. *Lady Lawyer*. New York: Robert Speller and Sons, Publishers, Inc., 1975.

Glunt, Ruth Reynolds. *Lighthouses and Legends of the Hudson*. Monroe, NY: Library Research Associates, 1975.

Glunt, Ruth Reynolds. *The Old Lighthouses on the Hudson River*. New York: Moran Printing Co., 1969.

Hassinger, Ernest, ed. "Official Souvenir Program: Old Home Week." Saugerties-on-the-Hudson, NY, July 1911.

Martin Cantine Company. *Fiftieth Anniversary Review 1888–1938*.

O'Callaghan, E.B. *Documentary History of the State of New York*. 4 vols. Albany, NY: Weed, Parsons, and Co., 1849–51.

Overbaugh, John S. and Donald Ringwald. "Saugerties Evening Line." *Steamboat Bill* 35, no. 1 (1978): 3–17.

Polk, R.L. ed. *Polk's Directory: Saugerties, NY*. New York: R.L. Polk and Co., Inc., 1928.

Saugerties, Ulster County, New York Maps. New York: Sanborn Map Co., May 1927.

The Sawyer. Saugerties, NY, 1913, 1945, 1947, 1950, 1953, and 1959.

"Souvenir Program of Grand Minstrel Carnival." Given by Snyder Hose Co. Band at Maxwell Opera House, 1908.

State of New York. *The Hudson-Fulton Celebration 1909*. Albany, NY, 1910.

Sylvester, Samuel Bartlett. *History of Ulster County*. Philadelphia: Everts and Peck, 1880.

Toodlum Tales. Saugerties, NY: Lith-Art Press, 1979–1980.

Ulster County Business Directory. Syracuse, NY: Hamilton Child, 1871–72.

Wachter, Evelyn Sidman. The Mansion House, Saugerties, NY. 1996.